About This Book

This book is about finding the sunshine! Even while the cold darkness of a life storm is in full force and stripping you of all your expectations, try to look for the sunshine. As the winds are increasing and you feel the force throwing you in all different directions, my hope is that this book will bring you foundational peace by helping you get a new perspective on what is happening in your life.

As life's battles stretch our core beliefs to the point of snapping and bring emotions like anxiety and doubt to the surface, fear of the unknown can become overwhelming. This book will allow calmness to take over and help you navigate the storm.

When you are in the middle of the storm looking for hope through the heavy rains, embrace the strength that is within you and see the sunshine that will guide you through life.

Life storms are inevitable and are designed to strip us, stretch us and strengthen us so that we find our purpose in life and surround ourselves in warm sunshine.

Dedication

This book is dedicated to the brightest sunshine in the world, Samantha Kaywood.

As well as to all the family and friends that have experienced her “sunshine”. To those that have embraced her for what she has to offer this world and chose to learn and grown from her.

I hope this story of what she has taught me, can in some way, help you find your strength through the storms of life.

May you be stripped, stretched, and strengthened and be embraced by the sunshine.

Table of Contents

Chapter One

Life Happens

I knew I was having a girl because of the amniocentesis results. Super excited that she would be the first granddaughter in her dad's family. There were already 7 grandsons, so this was thrilling to learn she was a girl. When her dad's parents found out the news, it was like a bunch of pink balloons were bursting all over. Finally, a baby girl is on the way.

The joy measure dial was at an all-time high knowing the first girl was on her way. As visions of pink, girly dresses danced in my head, the thought of why I had to have an amniocentesis escaped all my brain waves.

I had to have an amniocentesis because a test result suspected Down's syndrome or spinal bifida.

There I was lathered up with the ultrasound gel as the tech located the baby, she washed my belly with a cold cleansing solution. Having total trust and faith that the tech knew exactly what she was doing, I did everything as instructed. She said, “arms to your side”. My arms went to my side like I was a robot following orders. “Take a deep breath and let it out slowly you will feel a cramp”. She was not kidding. It did not feel like a cramp, no way. Even though the slender needle entered my belly button, it felt like a rush of razor-sharp needles were cutting my insides. Then a rush of electrical zapping was causing pressure and pain. I had no idea how dangerous this procedure could have been. It was over quickly, and the pain and pressure all cleared up as soon as the needle was taken out with the sample of fluid.

After a dreadful 48 hours of fear, doubt and praying. I repeat, fear, doubt and praying, the amniocentesis results were all clear they said, and I was having a girl!

We decided her name would be Samantha. Samantha because of this super sweet girl that was a grade ahead of me in school. She had long straight beautiful silky brown hair. She was always purely innocent and kind. She was also extremely talented at not getting involved in drama. I had a deep attraction to her peace.

February 22, 1995 Samantha blesses this world with her arrival via scheduled induction. I remember hearing her crying as the doctor placed her on my stomach and cleaned her up. That moment, there she was crying, and squirming and I had no idea what was next. I quickly went through my brain files of all the books I read to prepare for this moment. I got nothing! I thought wait, what was in that epidural, did it block my brain too? Then I realized, all the books I read, were about "what to expect when I was expecting"! How could I be so unprepared and not read about what to expect after the expecting arrives?!?!??

The strong, confident, in a hurry nurse asked me "bottle or breast?" I was like um yea breast that is the best right? She looked at me with this disciplined voice and said, "go ahead then". I just looked at her with confusion.

She began approaching me, closely. I thought she was going to get in the bed with me, she was coming so close. While she was way up in my space, she grabbed the crying baby and stuck her on me to start nursing.

It was like a piranha grabbed a hold of me and was chewing me up! For those of you who have breast fed you feel me right? The nurse said wow, “she's a good baby” she nurses so well. Those words “she's a good baby” meant as compliment, would soon become a pain trigger.

I remember swaddling her up in blankets to take her home and noted on the paperwork her apgar scores were 9 and 8. Apgar is a score test given to newborns after birth. This test checks a baby's heart rate, muscle tone and other signs to see if extra care is needed. A score of 10 is the best. They typically do 2 tests within minutes of each other. Samantha's scores were 9 then 8. Which indicated no extra care needed.

So off I was to take her to the car. Ok so I am certain some of you can relate to how awkward it is to take a fragile newborn and secure them in a car seat. She was so little, and the car seat just soaked her up. In comes my first "mom fear" experience. Man, mom fear can be brutal! The self-talk went something like this. Her neck is so flimsy it is going to break on the first bump. Ok let me put rolled up blankets around her to secure it. No wait what if she turns her head sideways, she will suffocate before I get home. Ok wait I will sit in the back seat and hold her head up. Yes, that is a great idea. Ok great got that taken care of. So, she is buckled in, I am right beside her supporting her head and her dad starts driving. So, yea mom fear had arrived and now momma bear woke up. As her dad started to drive, he could not do anything right. I mean if he was not going too fast, he was going too slow and either way it was going to cause a wreck. He could not control the temperature well enough in the car and of course that was going to lead to hypothermia. When he decided music would help calm the mood and probably drown my nagging out, I snapped! Oh, yea full-bore head-on snap and the lion arrived! I let all my fear, doubt, anxiety, worry etc. just come out like a roaring lion at him. Poor guy did not have a chance. His eyes got big like he was staring the devil smack in the face. Thankfully, we arrived home safely shortly after that.

We got her out of the car and up into the house. As I took her out of the car seat carrier, I noticed her neck was "stuck" to one side. It was so stiff. I thought back to when we were at the hospital and I could not remember her neck being that way. Yep, sure enough Mom guilt arrived. For those of you who know who she is, you clearly understand how sick at your stomach she can make you. For those of you who do not know her, let me introduce her to you. Mom guilt can quickly show up at any time out of nowhere. When she arrives, it is like you have been punched in the stomach.

Sometimes the punch even takes your breath away. Then she starts with the negative talk, judging, complaining, degrading etc. She is brutal on a light day and can be downright paralyzing on a heavy day.

So, on this day I was introduced to mom guilt as the negative self-talk began. Oh no did I break her neck by supporting her head too much? Did I wrap her too tight? Did I hold her on the wrong angle? What will people think of me? What would her dad say to me? How do I fix this? I am a bad mom I am no good at this. I am a failure! There it is, there is the devastating lie mom guilt strives to get us to believe in. The lie that we are failures at being moms.

So, there I was sick to my stomach, negative chatter from mom guilt, a baby with a stuck neck and me a nurse with absolutely no clue what I am going to do or how I'm going to do it. I had nothing, no solutions. As the feeling of my upset stomach began to travel back up my throat, I quickly did what most new moms do. I called my mom sobbing bless her heart.

How awful it must have felt for her to be on the other end of the phone miles away hearing her baby sobbing and unable to be there to "fix it."

Us moms are programmed like that. To "fix It". I believe dads have the "fix it syndrome" as well. The dad "fix it syndrome" however, comes with so much more power to defeat and destroy any type of confidence. It can cause the dad to run or back off and let the mom "fix it syndrome" have the control. I believe it is a coping mechanism that happens as an attempt to help the mom feel better or vice versa if the mom back offs, she is attempting to allow and hoping the dad "fixes it". Either way the blame game can make an appearance as another attempt to feel better from feeling inadequate.

My mom talked to me, kept me off the edge and gave me tons of support that it was fine. More importantly she was heading over to help me and that was so comforting. For some reason, the presence of parents, calms us down which allows us to see clearly and solve our issues. That human unconditional love and support that helps us rise, overcome, conquer, etc.

I believe parents gain this unexplainable confidence as they raise their child, especially a woman. That confidence grows as they raise their 2nd,3rd and so on. You can see it just take over and take charge when a grandmother shows up to assist. That can be good when the new mom is overwhelmed or bad if the power struggle starts.

So, there I was instantly calm as my mother arrived to assist with that strong confidence I had never noticed before. I remember thinking wow she is impressive. Wow she really knows what to do. I was wowed because it was at that moment, I realized how sorry I was for treating my mother with disrespect when I was pregnant.

I was still suffering from teenage know it all syndrome, even though I was in my twenties. You know the syndrome where the teenager is 100% certain their mother does not know, could not possibly understand what we are going through. Teenagers get that mentality and never stop to realize their parents were teenagers once too. No, all the teenagers think is they do not know, and our times are different. However, life will always prove history repeats itself.

I remember that moment, there I was supposed to be all prepared with all the books

I read while being pregnant. I felt in a total daze as I watched my mother with an 8th grade education whom I had no idea could help me, take full control of the baby, me, and the house. True champion right there. That was the day I graduated from the teenage syndrome into the grateful new mom phase. I could not thank my mom enough. I could not stop apologizing either, for my judgmental, condescending attitude. So yep, you guessed it. Not only was mom guilt in the room now I welcomed regret to the party too. I was slowly brewing a postpartum depression cocktail.

So, after a while and I was calm, I showed mom Samantha's neck. She thought it was just stiff but to make sure and get ideas, she called her lady squad. Yea lady squad. So, my mom's common-sense ability is off the chart it is so good. She will say to this day, "well common sense told me". So, her common sense told her to call her lady squad and see if they ever seen a neck like this. After several calls she was certain it was just stiff from being in the womb and will work itself out. What a relief!

The next day the home nurse came out to do a home visit for me and baby Samantha. She too agreed with my mom and felt it was nothing. No additional care needed to be done about it. She did tell me to mention it to Samantha's pediatrician on her well baby checkup. So yes, you guessed it. I immediately called the pediatrician to schedule that well baby checkup. That poor receptionist that answered the phone had no idea the size of the basket case she had on the other end. So, like many, when I get upset or worried it comes out in a strong anxious kind of tone. Topped with a little protective momma bear attitude. You picking up what I am talking about? I know some of you moms know exactly what I am talking about.

There is this protective instinct that quickly rushes to the scene like a 911 ambulance when any indication of misinterpretation or accusation is made about our child. It is the finger waving, head swaying, oh no you did not just say that instinct!

The receptionist asked what type of appointment I needed. I said proudly “a WELL-baby checkup please”. She asked the name and date of birth of the baby. I again proudly gave her the information. Then she said “ok we can see her in 2 weeks would mornings or afternoons be best” she asked me. I calmly said “no 2 weeks is much too long. I need my baby checked today or tomorrow at the latest”. Then the attacks started. Well at least in my defensive, negative mind they were attacks because they created fear, doubt, and uncertainty in addition to guilt and feeling like a failure. “What's wrong with your baby?” she asked. I was like “excuse me”? She repeated “what's wrong with your baby”? Then she followed that up with stating” if you need to be seen sooner there must be something wrong with your baby why do you need her to be seen today or tomorrow”? I said “ok first know this, my baby is absolutely perfect and beautiful nothings “wrong” with her ma'am! I want her to be checked by the pediatrician to instruct me on how to help her neck that is all”. She asked, “what's wrong with her neck”? I answered in a raised voice “nothing! I just need her to be seen, could you please just stop your rude questioning and schedule that appointment for my perfectly fine baby”!

I mean seriously how silly did I just sound? At the time, my emotions were at an all-time high and they were not good emotions. They were full of fear, doubt, and disappointment. Of course, the poor receptionist was the punching bag of my emotions, maybe because I had so many fears of the unknown?

That is a mental breakdown cocktail starting to brew. She was quickly taken back, and I could sense she was not happy with my outburst. She replied with a date and time and said goodbye.

The sunshine from Samantha is, life happens as it should, and it is preparing us. What if we need this storm of emotions, circumstances, mountains, and valleys so that we are prepared for the next chapter of life? What if, this preparation is part of our life's purpose?

Chapter Two

Unexpected Landing

There I sat with my cute, adorable, good baby waiting on the pediatrician to come see her and assure me all was well. Then the nurse walked in. "Good morning. What brings you in to see the doctor today" she asked?" "The home nurse suggested I get confirmation from the doctor that Samantha's neck was just stiff, and it is nothing to worry about", I answered.

The nurse took notes, then got Samantha's weight and did some measuring of her head and such. She wrote notes again.

Ok so being a nurse I totally understand, from it being drilled in our heads, that if we did not chart it, we did not do it. From day one in nursing training, the mantra is chart, chart, and chart!

Even though I understood that, why was I getting anxious over the nurse charting? Why was this ugly conversation going on in my head? I was questioning what she was writing as if it were a bad note about Samantha. I was asking myself, what did she write down? It had better be all good! I was so defensive and uptight. Like I was to ready fight.

Looking back, I can now see it was the mom squad defense team that showed up in my head. You know what I mean right? The strong squad self-talk that says, there is not anything wrong MY baby. The attitude that makes a momma ready to fight, with any negative talk or thoughts about MY baby. Also known as the mom squad defense team.

As I write this out and I am taken back to that moment. I can feel the emotions as if it is happening right now. The anxiety is increasing as my body is beginning to go into fight mode. It amazes me how powerful our mind is. It can take us places mentally we have never been before. Those can be happy places or not so happy places, all with the power of self-talk.

At that moment, I must have had some type of intuition that I was up for a fight, right? Did I talk myself right into a negative hurtful battlefield?

The nurse left the room and you better believe It, I began searching for that chart of notes. It was like I was instantly searching for a weapon. I was opening each drawer and cabinet, being certain to close them quietly but rapidly. I had nothing, darn it. I could not locate those notes. Then, I realized, she took them with her. A sense of calmness started to take over and I was able to sit down, relax and begin to soak up baby Samantha. Is there anything more calming than an adorable baby looking up at you with a smile? I think not.

Suddenly, I hear a knock on the door and before I could say come in, the door was opening, and the doctor and nurse were walking in as if they were headed to some sort of race. In a hurry and on a mission was the feel in the room. The doctor introduced himself. He was average height, wore distinctive glasses, dressed very professional, with a long white medical coat on, as doctors do, and had a strong handshake. "Hello there," he said, with his manly voice, to me. As he approached Samantha, he got a sweeter voice as he addressed her, who was sleeping at this time. "hello baby Samantha", he whispered in that gentle voice.

Once he realized she was sleeping, he pulled up a chair and sat right next to me and asked “what brings you in, as it's too soon for a well-baby check? “

I answered, “oh yea, the home nurse suggested I get confirmation from you that nothing is wrong with Samantha's neck”. He asked me to let him see her. I got her out of her carrier and handed her gently to him all swaddled up in those soft baby receiving blankets. As she began to open her eyes and squirm, she did not cry one bit. He proceeded to unwrap her from her blanket. Still no crying and he said that statement “wow she's a good baby”. He began to examine her neck and of course I am standing right beside him overlooking every move he makes right? Why? You guessed it, 1st time mom syndrome. It is the syndrome that causes moms to be overprotective and over worry and carry an attitude as a weapon. All us mothers and caregivers know exactly what I'm talking about right? I was watching him try to manipulate her neck and I could see her starting to grimace as if it hurt. You better believe I stood straight up, like a cat's hairs would in a ready to protect situation and touched his arm, like stop, what are doing without saying a word. I am certain the tight "touch/grip" I had on his arm, made him sense I was uncomfortable. He stopped and wrapped her back up. Then he held her and consoled her a few minutes so she would not start to cry. Which totally melted my heart.

His eyes directed me to sit down so he could hand this tiny fragile newborn back to me. I could tell by the look on his face he was about to tell me something he did not want to tell me. The fear and worry were increasing because as he was examining her, and I was looking over his shoulder I could tell her neck appeared to stiffer than the day before. He grabbed his chair and sat next to me again. He asked" is anyone with you today"? I said "no just me and Samantha". He took a deep breath and with a confident voice and look said "ok, from the examination of Samantha's neck she has a condition that we call torticollis. It is a rare condition in which the neck muscles contract, causing the head to twist to one side. This can and most likely will resolve on its own without treatment". He then said, "you have a beautiful special baby."

I was totally ok with what he said. This doctor's confidence made me totally trust him. He gave me the name and number of the local Children's hospital to get set up for physical therapy. He felt the physical therapy would help the neck muscle loosen up.

Several weeks went by and Samantha was doing very well with feedings and sleeping. I learned she was a spitter. A baby that spits up a lot after eating. I would make sure she always had a bib on. I can remember that milk spit up smell. Like a cross between a sweet baby smell and sour milk. I felt like that was my perfume. I seem to always have spit up on me and smell like that.

As time passed by, I kept looking at her baby book milestones and waiting for her to reach them so I could proudly put the information in her book. I never had a baby book, that I knew of, so I wanted to make sure Samantha had an incredibly detailed book we could go through someday together and share memories, when she became a mother.

When Samantha was about 3-4 months old my mother and I were going through the baby book. I was getting concerned because I was not able to fill out the book with dates for rolling over and finding her toes. As the concerned gained intensity, my mom, who started to wonder as well, put Samantha on the floor to play with her. My mom loves to play with kids. Even today, in her 70's she still loves nothing more than to make a child smile. She is an awesome playmate too because she is still a child at heart. As she began to play with her, she said to me "Debi, I think she's tracking the toys with her ears instead of with her eyes". I asked what she meant? What are you saying mom? She said I think we should have her seen by an eye doctor and get her vision checked. I suddenly felt the defensive, I am going to prove you wrong attitude, show up. Somehow it fueled me on a mission to prove to the world that nothing was wrong with my child. It was like it was a reflex reaction that I could not control. Looking back, I wonder if my intuition suspected something? I mean while I was pregnant and happy as can be that I was going to be a mother, a bomb went off from a blood test with 50% accuracy that my baby may or may not have a deformity. It was like that moment planted a seed of doubt. Over the next several months that negative seed was watered by having to be introduced to torticollis and now this possible visual issue. Both of which were now feeding the doubt that I could not produce a healthy baby. I was even doubting my ability to be a mother, wife, friend, etc. I was on a mission though to prove everyone wrong that had any doubt, including myself. My ego was in full control and fired up.

I hate to admit that I even had any doubt, but looking back, I can see I had a ton of it, and it was soaking up my happiness.

I started the intense research to get an appointment with the top eye doctor at children's hospital. We are so fortunate to have one of the best children's hospitals in the eastern part of the USA. Mission accomplished as we got scheduled with the head of the ophthalmology department. I was super excited I managed to pull that off.

So, the day of the appointment came, it was on a Friday, and of course my momma was with me for that support she is always giving out. The doctor assessed her vision and said we need to get a CAT scan. I did not even question why, at that moment, I totally trusted that this doctor knew exactly what to do. I was super impressed he was able to get the scan the same day. So off to cat scan we went, and it went smooth as butter. After the scan was complete, they told me Samantha's pediatrician would be in touch to explain the results. My mom and I walked out of children's hospital that day feeling very accomplished. Mission complete with a bonus of a cat scan the same day. Little did I know my world was about to get dark.

We got a call that Sunday, yes, I repeat, on a Sunday from the pediatrician. They asked if both me and Samantha's father could come in to discuss the cat scan results. I was quick to reply yes and set up a time. I called Samantha's father and told him the doctor wanted to see us. We both said it felt weird that they wanted us to come in on a Sunday. The ride to the doctor's office was only 15 minutes away but man it seemed like it took hours. I could feel anxiety increasing as we walked into the waiting room where there was only us and the nurse. She took us right back and sat us down at the doctors' desk.

Now up to this moment I was having concerns yes, but I was still on cloud 9 of becoming a mother. I was in defensive mode at times but still felt like I was on my way. Suddenly, as the doctor said Samantha has a brain anomaly, I felt like I had just had a crash nosedived landing. I instantly felt like I had landed in the wrong destination, on a flight, with nothing but darkness and negativity surrounding me. Like I landed in a world I was not supposed to be in.

Of course, Samantha's Dad bombarded him with questions. Questions were being asked like what does this mean? How can it be fixed? Is she in pain? How would this happen? Why did this happen? I knew though, from my medical background, exactly what a brain anomaly meant. It meant part of her brain was missing and brain damage is most likely.

As I sat and listened to the questions and answers my brain was instantly searching for answers as my stomach kept getting more and more upset. Then I heard what do we do now? I peeked up to hear the answer. The doctor said you go see a neurologist at children's neurology department, they will guide you.

As we picked up Samantha and headed back home trying to still swallow the forever life changing news we just received, all I could think, and feel was lost and defeated. There is something wrong with my baby.

I began reviewing my whole pregnancy trying to see where I messed up. The blame game began. First, I blamed myself. How could I not have been healthier? I am a nurse I should have known better. This had to be because I was not a healthy eater. Then it was on to blame others. Who might you ask? You name it I blamed them. As we started to tell our family and close friends, I noticed they all looked to me for answers. Not sure if that was because I was the mother or because I was a nurse. Either way, I had nothing but guesses. I wanted to know the answers though.

It was like I had planned a trip to Italy. I read all the books, learned the language, purchased all the proper clothing but landed in Germany a deep dark cold place. I did not know the language. I was not prepared by no means and had no sense of how to go on.

Imagine being in a dark, closed circular room with no doors. I began a 2-year long journey of trying to ease my way around the walls of this circular room looking for a door to get out. It was not supposed to be like this. I was supposed to have a healthy happy baby. The blame had left, anger came and went, and depression planted a deep strong weed in my soul.

I was so broken deep to my core. I would tell myself I did this, I created this and I better "fix" it! Fix what? Fix Samantha. Everyone was depending on me to "fix" it.

I asked the neurologist what her diagnosis was? He replied with, she has several. A small head also known as microcephaly which may cause delayed development. She is missing a part of her brain that separates the right and left hemispheres called the corpus callosum. There was probably a shift in her brain that caused some brain damage because the corpus callosum was missing. She will most likely develop some visual delays centrally called cortical visual impairment due to the optical nerve having damage. She will probably be able to see peripherally just not centrally. Her tone in her arms and legs are over toned and her stomach is under toned which indicates mobility issues. We typically call this a multi handicap situation with a generalized diagnosis of cerebral palsy. Now cerebral palsy was something I had heard of before and I knew that could mean a wide range of disabilities. I remember asking the neurologist what does her future look like? He answered, "her future depends on your involvement".

The World Wide Web was just becoming trendy. I would search and apply for everything the neurologist told me to do. After 2 years and maxing out our health insurance, we were granted a county "waiver". That waiver allowed me to get help caring for Samantha. Day cares would not enroll her due to her diagnosis, but health care agencies could send help. The first agency sent a true angel to us named Dodie. She taught me one of the most valuable lessons in my life. She could see my pain and sadness daily. She taught me to quit searching for the door to get out. I was exactly where I was supposed to be, and God blessed me with Samantha he did NOT punish me. She taught me Samantha was not broken and I did not have to "fix" anything. All I had to do was go to the center of the room and I would find a sunshine like no other. She will teach me exactly what I need to learn in this life. I did exactly that and I found my Samantha Sunshine.

The sunshine from Samantha is we are not broken. We are exactly who we were designed to be.

Chapter Three

The Advocate Road

Once I realized that I was broken, not Samantha, I got this unexplainable drive to get over the "what about me" syndrome. Now my focus was to be Samantha's advocate. Have you heard of the "what about me syndrome"? It is when we get stuck with a mentality of poor me, what about me, it is so hard on me. As if we are the only ones in this world going through the storms of life. I call it the "what about me syndrome". I knew I had been depressed and stuck for a while. When my mind shifted from trying to get out of my situation to seeing that I am exactly where I am supposed to be and this baby needs me, that what about me syndrome disappeared. Poof, just like that a simple mind shift was one of the most powerful moments in my life! It was like a superhero power was implanted in my soul. Watch out Batman here I come. Suddenly, I was on a mission not to "fix" her but give her every opportunity to be the best version of Samantha she could possibly be. Little did I know, that in that process I would also find the best version of myself.

So being Samantha's advocate began. I had to begin being her voice since she could not speak. I had to look at the situation and decide will this test, or procedure help improve her life quality or not? Would the test the medical team wanted to do be worth the pain and suffering? I remember a time when I kept telling the doctors she is still spitting up a lot and it did not seem right. She would spit up and start to choke. They did an EGD (esophagogastroduodenoscopy) that is where a scope is put down your throat to look at the esophagus, the stomach and first part of the small intestine. They found no abnormalities and had no explanation as to why she is spitting up and choking. Then the neurologist suggested a sleep study and thought maybe this was a type of seizure activity. That was totally not obvious and made no sense to me, but I trusted him. So, we attempted a sleep study. For those of you who had the crown of glued wires from a sleep study, I am certain your mind can remember the heaviness. For those of you who have never had one, picture a head wrapped in gauze with wires coming out the top, resembling a mummy. They put electrodes all over your scalp, attach them with some type of "hair glue" and then expect you to sleep so they can monitor your brain waves. Now add a child that has sensory issues to the equation. You can imagine that it was like we were in a screaming and kickboxing match. I was holding her in a reclining chair whispering and singing. When that did not work, I would shift and try something else. I would stand up and do the walk, bounce, rock dance. She did not have the mobility and development yet to coordinate a “reach up” and pull the wires off her head. Trust me, if she could have reached up and pulled them off, I believe she would have and thrown in a slap at me as well. She communicated the only way she knew how, screaming and kicking. Seven long hours of her and I battling hard upstream at each other. I had to keep her calm so she would sleep, and a test result would appear. So many times, I wanted to throw the white towel in and run, run, run like Forrest Gump out of that place. She could not go to sleep long enough for the test to see anything of value. Nor could I sleep. Lol, what a stressful and wasted event that was. However, looking back it was one of those milestone moments for me and my role as Samantha's advocate. When we went for our follow up with the neurologist, he suggested we go ahead and just try the seizure meds to see if they would help. To our surprise it worked! The spitting up and choking had stopped. His medical experience and knowledge led us to a nonconventional diagnosis of seizure disorder. Wow was I so amazed and thankful. Also relieved he did not make us go through another sleepless night of torture with the crown of glued wires.

You know in today's medical world it appears doctors do not have as much authority to decide like that because insurance companies regulate what they do by pathway flow charts. A pathway flowchart is like a chart that says if a patient has symptom A, it is approved to do this procedure. If they do not have symptom A but it appears like it is possible, they could develop symptom A, sorry no treatment is approved. This leaves medical professionals with their hands tied. Do you know of anyone that had that happen to them? I have an uncle who had an artery blocked however it was not blocked enough to "qualify" for a stent. So now he must walk around on eggshells knowing the block is there and not fixed. How scary that must be. The insurance companies act as if we are all the same person and react to treatment the same. I am thankful we are all our own individuals because the world needs us that way. Wouldn't you agree? What if we all began advocating for ourselves, family, and friends? Oh yes, I believe we would start a movement in this world in the direction of individualized care. Advocating is powerful.

I had to learn to advocate for Samantha not only in testing, medications, treatments etc. but also in getting services and support. At the age of one, we had used her lifetime maximum allotment for speech, physical and occupational therapies. This sent me on my next role of investigator. Yup I became an investigator with a huge magnifying glass looking for clues under ever rock possible, to help her get the support she needed. This to me, is something most parents end up doing for their child at some point in their life, right? Investigate the best sport to lead them to or the best career path etc. Did you ever think your children would teach you so much? Maybe, all this teaching was preparing us for what was to come? Absolutely, it was. Everything happens in life to prepare us for what is to come.

So, let me explain the situation. Samantha was now going to 3-4 types of therapy 5-6 times per week. She was also still being treated by her neurologist and still being testing in developmental rehab to help her conquer the motor skills needed to progress in motor development. All these services added up quickly. Like I said earlier, we had reached the lifetime maximum amount for her and was starting to get denial letters from insurance. So, I began applying for assistance from the local, state, and federal agencies. I asked anyone I could for insight on assistance and applied for every one of them.

This was so hard for me to do. You see as a child I was raised by a single mother on welfare, which was so embarrassing to me. I can remember my mom being so stressed out every year during the renewal phase. She would worry we would not get approved, and we would not have food, electric, a home or water. I hated seeing her worry like that and always promised myself and her, I would never depend on the government for assistance. I would take every opportunity of learning a skill or trade to always work and support me and my family. Never in my wildest dreams would I have ever thought my insurance from working in my professional career would “max out”. That maxing out then forced me to go back to the welfare department begging for help with my tail between my legs. When I began thinking about going to the welfare department, sure enough, failure and depression were there ready to greet me and pull me back in. I mean I thought I was prepared! I earned a college degree! At this point in my life, I held 3 professional licenses! Why, oh why, must I be forced to go beg again? The feeling of defeat about stopped all progress for me. I was feeling nauseated and disgusted to the point of even considering not applying and stopping Samantha's services. Crazy thoughts huh? I was putting my fear and pride before my child's needs. I did feel like the world was against me and I was carrying the weight of Samantha's future upstream with heavy weights on my back. I did a quick mind refocus and some self-talk reminding me this is about Samantha. This is not about me and my pride and ego, this was about serving and helping my child have the best life possible! That mindset shift filled me up with motivation and emptied me of all pride and ego. It continues to amaze me at how powerful our minds are. We can shift our thinking and make our bodies follow. Reminds me of the saying. Where the mind goes the body follows. I implanted in my mind that Samantha had been placed in my care and I have a responsibility. So onward solider I marched into the application process and turned my frown upside down. I did not let fear stop me. I decided to break up with fear, doubt, pride, ego etc.

I can remember the day I was sitting in the welfare department, where I had sat with my single mom, in despair knowing I earned too much money to receive services. I was trying to defend my case as I explained the circumstances. I could see the case manager's sad face as she knew she could not help me but wanted too so badly. Then I heard a whisper from outside the cubicle. A lady that worked at the welfare department whispered to me "ask about the waiver program". I thought I was hearing things. So, I did not respond. For a moment I thought I was losing my mind and hearing voices. Then I heard it again and I peeked outside the cubicle and there she was whispering it again "ask about the waiver program". I did not hesitate, and I quickly leaned back into the cubicle and said to the case manager "what's the waiver program?". She looked up and with excitement said yes oh yes, the waiver program could be the answer. The rush of hope filled my spirit as I looked back to thank the whispering lady, but she was gone. Just like that she disappeared as if she was an angel. I had to recheck my sanity again, lol. I was not losing it though. She "The angel" was a lady who overheard our conversation and by listening to her spirit and with a huge caring heart she stepped out in faith to help me. Can you imagine what our world would be like if we all, without question or doubt, listened to our inner spirits? That moment was the beginning of a golden ticket for Samantha and our family. She was approved for the waiver because of her disability and my success with my earnings did not impact it at all. To this day the waiver is still serving and blessing us.

Even though Samantha has "special needs" life's experiences of the ups and downs are experienced by all parents and people. I can remember having some stinking thinking where a pity party would try to get started. I would think I was the only one going through all these tests, doctor appointments, trips to the hospitals, sleepless nights, etc. I know now we all have storms of life that strip us of our expectations, to stretch us to a breaking point, so we are strengthened for the journey. Yes, strengthened for the journey. I am sure you can think back right now of a time in your life when a storm of life felt like a devastating tsunami. Maybe you too, felt like life was sucking you under water with little pockets of air. Look at us now though! We survived, we learned, and we grew right? No room for stinking thinking. We must quickly reset the mind, refocus, and shift it to prevent the stink.

The sunshine from Sam is the desire to help others, is part of our makeup. It is a good thing. So just do it and let the sunshine in

Chapter Four

Shifting

Working 12-hour nights and therapy during the day was beginning to make my body fight back. I would try to function on less than 3 hours of sleep. Let me tell you when I do not get my sleep it is like the sweetness in me evaporates and all bitterness arrives. I bite back like a snapping turtle with every word spoken to me. Some might call it the sleep deprived monster. Maybe it is like going a week without coffee for those who love coffee. You feeling me now? This was going on for over a year when I decided enough is enough. Giving up therapy was not an option because Samantha's development depended on my involvement. How was I going to keep up with this pace? How could I possibly be able to earn an income while being expected to work by the hour? After many conversations with Samantha's father, we decided we would take our vacation earning side hustle and make a business plan that would allow us to have time freedom for Samantha. We first busted our debt with a strict pay off plan and then put goals in place that would allow us to work for ourselves full time. This opportunity would become one of the biggest pieces of Samantha's success while at the same time preparing me. The plan took some head down, hardworking drive with grit to accomplish. We had a huge why though and we both knew there was no other option. Just like you mothers and fathers out there, you do what you must do for your children or pets and somehow that inspires us right? We figure things out by looking under rocks for answers. No matter how heavy the rock or task we lift it, we get our answers, and we conquer. All because of unconditional love! So, Samantha gave us the wings to fly one amazing trip of having time freedom from being an entrepreneur. Funny how we go through things in life like a chapter of a book. Each chapter teaches us new skills and mindsets to prepare us for the next. There I was with a college degree in science, a registered nurse license, a cosmetology license, and a notary license, yet I was earning my living by designing landscapes, bookkeeping, accounting, marketing, sales, human resources, etc. Just like anyone of us with a strong passionate why it motivates us beyond what we ever thought we could do right?

Samantha's paternal grandfather had a mind like an engineer, and he would design and modify all types of equipment to help her have the best chance at life. What a blessing that was to her. One day he suggested I consider giving Sam a playmate. A man of little words just said some heavy strong words to me. Instantly I felt the core of my stomach start to churn with anxiety. The unknown of all the what ifs. You ever do that to yourself? Our minds quickly take over with the "negative what if's" to discourage, derail and destroy an idea or thought that could be very impactful and needed. So, he planted a seed of a possible second child. I ran through all the scenarios and thought well I have all the equipment; I have an understanding on how to advocate and I trust that man so why not. Without discussing with any doctors, Samantha's father and I agreed it would be a good idea, so we got pregnant with baby number 2 with absolutely no problem and no delay. As I began to announce the news to Sam's doctors, they were uptight with why I would do this without knowing what caused Samantha's delays. I was like wait, what? I thought we would never know, as I questioned the dr. He replied with well yea we may never know but he highly suggested genetic testing to prepare us. Hi ho hi ho off to more testing we go.

When we scrape ourselves an open wound appears right? It will bleed, cause some pain, and need time to heal and scab over wouldn't you agree? Well, the wound I created inside of me was as big as me and felt more pain than anything I'd ever experienced, because it was my broken heart. Broken heart from Samantha's birth expectations. You know what I am talking about? That, why does life have to go on, feeling? That, why me feeling? That, I cannot do this, feeling? Where can I run to feeling? Where can I hide forever feeling? You been there too? Time has no empathy that our world just got flipped inside out and upside down. Nope none, time just keeps on ticking into the future. Like water in the river keeps flowing. We too must keep ticking and flowing. As we exist through life though a miraculous thing happens. Life begins to drop a few “happy cells” in us. Maybe a new baby is born, a beautiful sunset or sunrise takes our breathe away or a dear friend sits and listens. A connection with nature and others becomes steppingstones in our healing and a scab starts to form. A hard scab becomes a protective covering over the wound. Healing happens one layer at a time.

As the wound from Samantha's initial diagnosis had now scabbed over, I could feel some pull on it as I got excited to have answers. I mean really was I excited about having answers? No, I had regressed back to wanting to know who to blame for this. I was sucked back into thinking I was a victim and Samantha was broken. I had taken a flight of stairs backward in my healing process. As it would be, the testing revealed nothing but rule outs. What are rule outs? That is when medical tests are perform to "rule out" suspected conditions. What we did learn was that Samantha's condition was not caused by any type of genetic condition that they could see from those tests.

The pregnancy with baby 2 was considered "high risk" because of my past with Samantha and no concrete answers. I now had to add a weekly visit to the baby doctor in addition to all the therapy appointments. They quickly located a potential kidney deformity to top it off. I mean I was already full of fear, stress, and anxiety of the unknown, and this new "advanced" high tech ultrasound picked up an early detection.

Now let us think about this for a moment. What can the medical professionals do with this information at this stage of the pregnancy? Can they fix anything during the pregnancy? Are they certain the new high-tech machine is accurate? It is my understanding now, that these tests are intended to help prepare the medical team and parents of any potential issues. Had I been a more in tuned advocate, I would have asked more questions about this test.

Questions such as, what will this test show about the baby and me? If a potential problem is found, what are the anticipated treatment plans? At that point, I could make a more informed decision whether to have the test or not, based on if I would be willing to do the anticipated treatment plans. However, I was not that in tuned with my advocating skills, like I said earlier.

So, there I was, already the parent of a special needs' child, pregnant with baby 2 without knowing what caused Samantha's disabilities. Now, I have increased worry and stress from a new "advanced" high tech ultrasound indicating a potential kidney deformity even though it had a high rate of false information, I later learned.

I did not keep a journal like I did with Samantha instead I was going to just embrace and experience the moments. A therapist once advised me to quit looking back at that baby journal I kept with Samantha, trying to "figure it out". She encouraged me to instead, capture each moment now as she experiences them. To this day, I am still recording those moments and celebrating each one of them. That intentional action right there, keeps the sunshine and hope in my heart that Samantha is still growing and developing.

The first-time baby 2 kicked it was not a "flutter" it was like a drum of feet kicking to get out. Wow was baby 2 active. Throughout the whole pregnancy it felt as if there was gymnastics going on inside of me. There were times my whole belly would roll from one side to the next like a somersault was happening. That was so exciting to experience all that movement. With Samantha there was movement, but it was always slow and subtle. It totally made sense too that baby 2 was so active, why? Because on November 7, 1997 the "son" that was supposed to be born with a malfunctioning kidney bounced out a healthy baby girl ready to take life on and tumble through it. All bodily functions were perfect, and the worry of her kidney malfunctioning was wrong. Totally wrong! All they worry and stress for no reason. They knew this because, as soon as she came out, she showed them her kidneys worked simply fine by peeing all over the doctor and pediatric specialist that was on site. They even had a helicopter on standby to transport the baby to Children's Hospital asap if need be.

Haley Elizabeth was born and not only was she going to teach me fast, but she was also Samantha's “Playmate For life” and would become quite the gymnast.

I can remember I use to set Sam on a blanket for belly time around 3-4 months old and she would stay there on her belly. So naturally I expected Haley to do the same. Not this tumbler, she rolled all over the place. I was not used to the quick development, but I got used to it quickly.

At this time Samantha was almost 2 and starting to pull herself but had not learned to stand up yet. So, it was like having twins. Double stroller, 2 car seats, 2 highchairs and both in diapers. As Haley quickly passed Samantha up in development, she became the role model. The therapists could see that Haley could get Sam to do any of the “play” workouts. Haley's curiosity led her to the toy and would say “come on Sam”. Sam was so full of smiles to play with her she would put her head down and work twice as hard to get to play with Haley. The smile Sam had and still gets to this day, after “playing” with Haley, lights up an entire room with soul shine.

One day Sam and Haley were supposed to be napping in their shared bedroom. I heard movement so I went in to check on them. Their grandfather, being the engineer type, had built a mini set of parallel bars to help Sam learn how to walk. Sam would not have anything to do with them except crawl through them. Well, on that day, I walked in to find Haley, the gymnasts, trying to do somersaults around one of the bars. As I corrected her and showed her what they were made for, she quickly started walking them and then encouraging Sam to do it. Sure enough, withing minutes, Haley had Sam up, holding on to the bars. I could not believe my eyes. I had tried so many times to get Sam interested in those bars. I attached toys, I stood at the end encouraging her to come to me and she would just freeze. However, once again Haley proved to be the motive for Sam's progression. Sam just adores Haley and her energy.

Haley has taken on the physical role of the "big sister" because she has grown and developed past Sam physically and mentally. What is crazy, is Haley has always seen Sam as her big sister and learns from her as well. She too gets a soul fill up when being around Sam, getting to snuggle with her and just laughing together. Haley continues to teach Sam new milestones in life by leading that example. She will continually help Sam develop new independent skills even though it scares this momma bear. Once again, no different than a typical sibling teaching session, right? Do you remember learning from your siblings? Have you watched your own children teach each other? Yet as adults, so many times, we miss the growing opportunity to learn, by blocking our thinking. We block it with the thought that learning from a child is not possible since we are the adults. A simple mind shift will open our minds to so much growth. I have learned that learning is a lifelong process.

So, Sam also has 2 younger siblings she was blessed with via a blended family. After Sam's dad and I divorced I was blessed with a high school classmate crush that God placed back into my life. He too was divorced and had 2 children. Their first introduction to Sam was life changing for them.

Imagine being around the age of 8 and 10 years old and your father just took you into a house where the 14-year-old could not talk well or walk very steady. Of course, you proceed with caution. Even though they were explained that she had delays from a condition known as cerebral palsy, that first encounter of seeing her had created a ton of fear. Fear of the unknown. The 2 of them clung to each other sitting as tightly as they could next to each other on the couch. I mean they were squeezing each other so tight I thought for a minute I seen white knuckles and knees. Even at that young age these 2 siblings were locked at heart, a tight connection for sure. As they got to know Sam and realized she was not going to hurt them they too found a natural playmate in her and began teaching her as well. They did not even know they were teaching her they just treated her like she was normal and encouraged her to do the things they were doing. Which is how my husband has always been with Sam. He sees her as Sam not as a child with delays.

Here is the crazy part, even though Sam is developmentally delayed she is still the oldest child. Through the years, when the other 3 siblings would battle frustration in their life, my husband and I, would remind them to "be like Sam". They would look at us with confusion and we would say it again "be like Sam". Sam is honest, quick to forgive and quick to apologize. See, if Sam naturally passes gas and you ask, "who farted?" most kids, out of embarrassment, will stay silent or quickly reply blaming others or saying not me, right? Sam on the other hand, says with her toddler speech delay, "I'm so sorry I farted I'm so sorry it stinks". Honesty in its purest form. She will also say "it's ok Debi" if I bump into her or get frustrated and raise my voice. When I apologize, she says "it's ok Debi" with a huge smile and tight hug. Quick to forgive and get back to loving each other. Now if Sam steps on you or does not follow directions and you redirect or correct her, she will quickly apologize. Not just once, no. She wraps her arm around your neck and says what's seems like a million times, "I'm so sorry Debi, I'm so sorry". It is with a genuine apology and sincerity that we are hurting, and she caused it. Bless her heart. Wow what simple lessons she can remind us of right?

I guess looking back Sam had the trait of "loving people" way back then I just did not see it until later. Sam will always pick playing with a person over a toy. People often ask me what would Sam want for her birthday? As my brain searches for answers the first answer was almost always "people" she would love to be around people more than a toy or gift. Here you have a child that cannot communicate well and is delayed in development yet being around people just makes her soul smile. That tells me people have an energy about them that can be felt. It would never fail, if we were in a crowd or at a get together, Sam would always find a shy quiet guy to go up to and plant those big brown eyes and sweet smile on. There have been times that the person she picked appeared to be a standoff person not interested and totally unapproachable. How does that happen? Energy and vibe? It is obvious to me Sam was able to sense that person's vibe of needing love and boom she was in it and pouring the love on. Makes me wonder if we used our energy vibe more often in our own relationships or around others if the connections would be different? Would there be more kindness? Would there be more love? If you have ever been hurt or disappointed emotionally, most of us have, a natural defensiveness starts that puts us into a protective mode. Maybe you have seen this or experienced it yourself? You meet a new person, engage in a conversation of curiosity, and start to question motives in your head? What if we were just open to allowing that person to be themselves? I believe it would change the way we see this world.

The sunshine from Sam is that people are exactly who they were meant to be. Love them, forgive them and be honestly open to allowing their life to impact ours. Choose love.

Chapter Five

Routine

At what point in our lives do we realize how important routine is? Am I the only one that did not figure this out until adulthood? I remember as a child, there were routines at school and routines at work. At that time however, I had zero appreciation for routines or how much of an impact they would have on me as a parent.

Sleep is priority number one as a new mother. Would you parents agree? I do not know about you, but I know my patience runs thin with less sleep. Sleep deprivation can lead to several undesired behaviors. Besides the common effect of lack of energy, it can also increase cravings for sugar and carbohydrates. You heard me right. This happens because our body needs quick energy. Unfortunately, that means it is burning sugar instead of fat.

Did you know that when our bodies do not get into deep sleep long enough it cannot do its full repair work? Instead, this causes an imbalance of our hunger hormones. It is not our fault when the baby's routine is off and causes us sleep deprivation that leads to overeating of bad choices and weight gain. This is what happened to me.

I could not eat enough and was constantly hungry. I craved donuts, pizza, sodas, carbohydrates, and sweets. Anything to "feel" better. I used food to fill my voids. As the weight increased so did the depression, health issues and low self-esteem. I was tired all the time. I found myself crying and exhausted constantly looking for something to help me.

This exhaustion led to napping when Samantha did. Ok so that reminded me of the kindergarten “nap time” back in the day. I just had a throwback to carpet squares and fighting to keep quiet during nap time. Seriously did we really fit on those carpet squares? Lol ok sorry about my “squirrel moment”. What I would give to have daily nap time now! Wouldn’t you? Think about It. What if there were nap pods at employment locations and we all got 15-30 minutes a day to nap and rejuvenate when we are sleep deprived? I can see that in our futures. Better yet, what if we just got good deep sleep every night?

I now realize that pregnancy is really training us to go on limited amount of sleep. Why do I say that? Because all parents now know, once the bundle of joy arrives sleep as we once knew it is over. Parents sleep patterns become defined by the child. We work with great intent daily to keep a routine all for the glory of sleep. I mean when the kids are sleeping and we parents are getting some "me" time, anyone that makes the littlest peep is going to get the stare down right? I had a neighbor that had a set of twins. She had a beautifully designed stern sign on her doorbell. It read, "kids napping, ring the bell and I will ring your face". We parents take nap time seriously, right?

Our routine is to get our children to use up energy so they will sleep, that becomes the focus of our life. We try anything that works. We even get ideas from other parents in hopes it will work for us. Get up, eat breakfast, play outside, eat lunch, nap only an hour or so or they will not sleep tonight right? Most parents will get what I am saying!

Having a "good baby" that slept through the night very quickly, was another blessing God gave me with Samantha. I did not need the "routine" thing, or so I thought. What I realize now is that as a new mother I needed time to learn all the tips and tricks to take care of my baby. Samantha's development delay gave me extra time to figure things out. Our schedule was working well for a while. Around 3 years old, she started waking up at 2:00am or sometimes 3:00am to start her day. This was much earlier than I wanted to start my day. Sleep deprivation can do some pretty bad things to one's attitude. Not to mention, the "what about me syndrome", and quick mean verbal attacks to innocent people. It is just not good lol. A whole year went by of asking one doctor after another what I could do. All I got was "it's a stage, she'll grow out of it". The question was if I would survive that long.

Finally, my support group mentioned to check the adenoids. I was very confused on how that would be causing her not to sleep.

Well, I learned if the adenoids are enlarged when a person lays on their back to sleep it could cause sleep apnea by blocking the airway. Sleep apnea is when a person stops and starts breathing in their sleep. Samantha had an x-ray where they determined her adenoids were enlarged and needed to come out. How thankful was I that I discussed the lack of sleep with the support group? Very thankful and appreciative that others wanted to help by making suggestions. Once the adenoids came out, the sleep increased, and this momma was smiling again.

This world has so many givers and helpers in it, all around us. To give is so fulfilling to our souls as well. Next time someone wants to offer help or a suggestion, be open to listening and maybe even accepting. The back and forth of giving and receiving is good for our souls and stability. I know I get embarrassed about my needs or concerns and sometimes I hesitate to talk about them. I also do not like to burden others with my responsibilities. That is just stinking thinking. It is not how we humans are designed. We are designed to serve and help one another.

I began noticing Sam hitting her head a lot with objects as if she were frustrated with something. I would run to her and try to figure out what was causing her to hit herself. This was a difficult task, because Samantha was still 80% nonverbal and using sign language. Her attempts at speaking were mostly sounds, but she could say 1 word clearly, mom. Yes, I was proud when she first said it, not going to lie. However, think about it, when that is the only word that can be said and people react to it, anyone would naturally use it often right? Well autism characteristics does not limit "often" in fact it becomes an obsession.

I can remember one trip to my sister, Donna's house with my niece Cortney and the 2 girls, Sam & Haley. Donna lived about an hour away, and the entire trip, Samantha kept saying "mom", "mom" "mom". At first Cortney and Haley thought it was funny. Funny, because I was getting annoyed. You would have too if you were mom, right? So, Cortney & Haley decided to start counting how many times she would say mom. Then they too got annoyed, and I believe stopped counting at around 300 times.

As Samantha grew physically, mentally she was still on a delay. Autistic characteristics started presenting more and more often. Especially when her routine was disrupted. What I learned was this is no different than most of us. We get use to a routine say going to work Monday - Friday. We get up at 5am for 5 days in a row, naturally our bodies want to get up at 5am on the weekend. When we decide not to get up at 5am and remain in bed trying to catch up on sleep, our routine is interrupted, and discord begins. There I go again infatuated with sleep! Seriously though, when the weekend comes a little something is stirred up when we get up later. It can be more difficult to make decisions while we deal with brain fog. Once we mentally get a handle on the plans of the day, we tend to regain grip and feel better. Samantha was no different. However, during that life stage, I had to fight feeling sorry for myself. Now there was the new diagnosis of autism that I had to start learning how to navigate with Sam. I had to go through accepting she had it, try to understand why and overcome depression and anger with a new mindset. If we think about it though, this cycle of acceptance is not unusual for most of us. Is it? As life throws us a change, we go through stages of anger, denial, depression and then acceptance. Wow, humans can get in our own way so much by being stubborn! I know I do.

Having a routine is still super important for Samantha. I got used to working my day around her schedule of eating, sleeping, therapy etc. When Samantha could not actually speak, I had to read her nonverbal cues when she was upset and try to put the puzzle together to figure out what was upsetting her. As she developed more and more, she began speaking in broken up sentences like charades. She would start with "Debi, um what's today yesterday Debi" and she would get stuck on a group of words like she was stuttering. She would keep saying it over and over until I would guess the end of a sentence. When I guessed right, she would say "yes! good job Debi" lol. We both would get excited when we got a sentence out and connected her thoughts to me. People ask me all the time “she calls you Debi instead of mom?” I explain yes, because one that is a typical autism trait and two, she hears everyone else call me Debi. Now there are times when she calls me Mom. Typically, she references me as “Mom” when she is upset with me and calling my Mom to tell on me. Yep, she calls me out. She calls my Mom and says “Mamaw, Mommy is being mean”. Of course, Mamaw does what any grandmother would do, she takes Samantha side and wants to punish me. I am so thankful my Mom is so good at comforting Sam. It has become routine that whenever Samantha is upset, sick or does not feel good, she has to call Mamaw and just her voice and unconditional support calms Samantha down. Another example of how important it is for us all to support one another. To listen and value each other, right?

Today Samantha can verbalize her wants more clearly even though she still struggles with weather she means today or yesterday. It is so beautiful to experience her being able to verbalize her wants and needs. As she progresses in her development, I can see her going through stages, just like a typical person does. The only difference is her physical age at the time of the development.

Let me explain. She is in a 26-year-old body yes, however mentally she flows between toddler talk and teenage talk. For example, every night before she goes to bed, she asks me “what's tomorrow going to be Debi?” I tell her she is going to the day program. She then asks, “who's coming tomorrow to put me on the van Debi?” After I tell her, she immediately asks “who is coming to get me off the van, Debi”. She wants to know, just like we all do, what is the next day’s plans right? Where is she going, who is coming to watch her, what is she packing for lunch, etc. On the days our routine changes, like the weekends, when the day program is closed, she gets upset and tells me “no Debi I have to go to the program”. I explain its closed and she immediately crosses her arms, pulls out the lower lip and pouts, just like a teenager not getting their way, right? I have found myself smiling and being excited when she talks back. Crazy huh? I smile and get excited because I see a new milestone being reached. That makes my soul shine. She is connecting her desires, to her brain and verbalizing! Simple and basic yes, but a reminder of the gift we are given to be able to feel, internalize, process, and project out in communication. There are many who cannot speak or communicate not because they do not want to, but because there is a breakdown in the physical ability to do so. Imagine how frustrating it would be to not be able to verbalize or communicate your frustrations, wants or desires? Maybe it would cause us to run from the frustration? Maybe it would cause us to hit ourselves or others? Maybe it would cause us to internally scream but unable for anyone to hear it? Autism is so hard to understand, but we are all still unique and have a right to be heard.

I know I take that for granted at times instead of soaking up someone's words as they use their gift of communication. Conversations today with people, are so much more interesting to me. Not only is the art of communication interesting but listening to their words, processing it, and feeling their spirit has become comforting as well as exciting to learn.

The sunshine from Sam is that routine keeps the mind calm. Communication is a gift, maybe we can see the value in it and appreciate it more often, keeping in mind some communication is not in words but in smiles and non-verbal body language.

Chapter Six

Gifts

How many times in our lives are we presented with a gift? Maybe a birthday is coming up? Your loved one decides they want to give you a gift. They start tossing ideas around in their heads. Maybe asking themselves, what would you like? What don't you have? Some people are so hard to buy for. They either have everything or we do not really know enough about them to pick a gift they will like.

For some people, gifts, are their love language. What is a love language? So glad you asked. There are 5 love languages that fill our love banks. They are time, touch, service, words, and gifts. Good news is, we all have them. Typically, we have 1-2 dominate ones that really fill our love bank. Giving and receiving gifts is one of them. For those that get filled up on this, it really means the world to them when someone takes the "time" to think of them and present them with a gift. Ironically, "time" is typically the 2nd dominant love language for those who get filled up on gifts. Which love language do you get filled up on? Here is a little hint, the one you tend to do the most is the one that is your dominant one. My love language is words. I totally enjoy encouraging others and cheering them on.

Personally, I also love to give to others. When a gift buying task is at hand, I find nothing but pure enjoyment, unless the funds are tight.

When funds are tight, I struggle at first with some negative self-destructing emotions. Like telling myself I should have enough, or I should make more money. Then I refocus my mind by being grateful for the money I do have and Pinterest! Every woman has either experienced Pinterest yippees or Pinterest yells. Most of mine are yells of discouragement because my gift project looks nothing like the picture. That puts a fun challenge on me to still give with my heart within my means.

How do you tackle your gift buying? Is it a chore or a joy? How do you feel inside when the person opening the gift really loves and appreciates your kind gesture?

Samantha has helped me to remember that gift giving and receiving are designed for both the giver and receiver. Not just the receiver and it is never really about the actual gift item.

Let me explain. Once Sam could say the words "thank you", around age 8 or 9, she started using them often. She would use them appropriately most of the time, but also inappropriately which was kind of fun. Imagine you are sitting around the table and someone sneezes. Suddenly, the silence is broken with Sam saying “fank you”. Yea you guessed it, the room filled with laughter as we instructed her to say “God bless you” but laughed with her. She would still use a toddler sound when saying “Thank you” so it sounded more like “Fank you”.

Of all the words to say she was saying “thank you”. That amazes me and makes my heart so happy to be reminded to say thank you. Everyone loves to feel appreciated. I know I do.

However, it was a couple of years later when I could see a new milestone being reached as Samantha mentally understood the words “fank you” and the emotion was now attached.

It was Christmas morning, and all the other kids were awake and waiting on Sam to wake up. It is ironic that she slept in. Samantha typically awakes on most days by 5:30am. Funny thing is Christmas is the only day Samantha would sleep in. Crazy, I know but true story. The other kids would often complain through the year at how early Sam would wake up and make sounds that would wake them up. The one day of the year they wanted her to wake up early, yet she would sleep in. Was this her way of teaching her younger siblings' patience? Maybe.

So, when Sam finally woke up, the kids were chopping at the bit to open gifts. The grandparents had arrived, Santa had left gifts under the tree and breakfast was fed. I mean breakfast was inhaled.

We all gathered in the living room in our spots to collect our gifts. The gifts were all handed out to each child. We have a tradition to open one gift at a time so we all can enjoy the gifts and emotion together. Of course, the other kids open their gifts fast. I mean lightning speed fast. You have seen it. Rip those papers off and swing it in the air. Open the box as quickly as possible with all kinds of paper and stuffing flying all over. The beautiful sound of unwrapping.

Sam, on the other hand, usually takes a longer time to rip the paper off and usually needs help opening the gift. On this year of discovery as it came to be Samantha's turn, we handed her a gift and said, “this is from Barbie & Jack”. Sam repeated what we said in a question “from Barbie & Jack?” I replied, “yea from Barbie and Jack open it up Sam”. Sam looked at the gift all wrapped up then looked around to see where Barbie & Jack were. She said “fank you Barbie & Jack, fank you so much, I love it”. She would say it with such heat felt sweetness and a huge smile would take over her face. Still to this day Sam gets nothing but huge smiles on her face during a time of gift giving and receiving. With all her heart she wanted to express how much she appreciated the gift, so she got up and walked over to them and hugged them both as tight as she could without hurting them. She again said "fank you fank you so much".

To all of us in the room, at first, we were laughing that she was doing this. The kids were encouraging her to open the gift. They wanted to see what it was. Sam loved the gesture of being given a gift so much that the gift did not really matter.

Then it hit us that her example of receiving a gift is how we all should be. You see, Sam had not opened the gift yet to even know what it was. She was so overcome with gratitude of a gift being given to her that before she even knew what it was, she was thanking and hugging.

A great lesson to be learned from a child with developmental delays huh. So many times, some children and some adults get so upset when they do not get the gift they expected. Where did that learned behavior come from? How could a developmentally delayed child not have the same issue? Not sure I have those answers, but I do know Sam had a lesson that we all could learn from. A simple lesson of gratitude.

Nowhere in the baby book, did I see stages of emotional development, such as gratitude, to monitor and record as a milestone to be reached. None of the books I read, or classes I took to prepare me to be a mother discussed emotional milestones either. How many times in our lives do we struggle with emotional development? As I watched Sam develop emotion and rationale behind a simple task like giving or receiving a gift, I began to appreciate emotions more.

Sam was able to defer her diploma at the age of 18. That means that due to her special needs, she qualified to stay in school until the age of 22. She would be in a class where they focused on activities of daily living and life after high school. So thankful for that program. Due to her delay, those years were extremely important for her development in activities of daily living. Everything happens for a reason, right? Ironically enough, several years prior to Sam getting into that program, another special needs mom and dear friend of mine introduced me to an incredibly special woman on a mission to serve the special needs community. She was the teacher at that program and taught Sam so many things. Not only about gift giving, but life skills including how to handle her menstrual cycle. Yes, I went there only because I get asked how I handle that time of the month so often. I cannot take any credit for Sam learning how to handle that. That was all taught by her teacher, bless her heart. To this day, Sam is amazing at changing those pads and of course letting everyone know she is on her period. She will say in a sad voice, “I am on my period”. Followed by “I hate wearing pads”. She keeps them on though, thanks to the routine and reminders taught by that incredible teacher. Teachers with hearts on a mission make this world a better place.

During Sam’s time in that program, her teacher would ask for a Christmas list of people Sam could buy for along with some ideas and money. In trying to build Samantha's skills in daily living, Christmas shopping, wrapping, and giving was a part of the training.

The first year she did this and had the gifts under the tree to give to her siblings and family she was so excited she had a hard time leaving them alone until Christmas Day. Isn't that interesting? Most of the time the kids are super excited to see what the gift is under the tree for them. Not super excited about the gift they will give away. She kept trying to get them to open the gift before Christmas.

When it was finally Christmas and her turn to give out her gifts, she literally wanted to help them unwrap the gift. The whole time she is handing the gift to her sibling she is smiling from ear to ear. She would stand as close as possible to them, invading all sense of personal space giggling with excitement. She does this shoulder shrug and sways her shoulders back and forth and up and down when she is excited and feeling the love. As they said, "thank you Sam" she almost had tears of joy as she replied with excitement "you're welcome, you're so welcome". The recipient would say "I love it" and Sam would reply with “I love you”. Wow! That is right Sam. Gift giving is really about LOVE. Expressing it in a unique way with a personalized item.

The sunshine from Sam is that gifts are items used to express love. Express love in both giving them and receiving them. Next time you are involved in a gift transaction remember to spread love all over it and not to fret too much over finding the “perfect” gift because the transaction of “giving” is the true “gift”.

Chapter Seven

Happy

Imagine you have just walked into the house and your dog realizes your home. Most of the time, you will experience some tail wagging. You might get some barks of dog love language or a jump up on you and lick your face. But one thing is for certain, they sure are glad to see you. No matter what kind of day you have had the welcome home, I love you wag from a pet always gives us some happy hormones.

How many times in our lives have we been given the "welcome home, I love you wag "to our family? Congratulations to those of you that may have mastered this skill! I know for me, my emotions can get in my way.

After a long day of up and down emotional heart tugs, coming home depleted and tired makes it a challenge. A challenge to have the mindset and energy to give the "welcome home, I love you wag".

Is that an excuse? Absolutely! Can I do better? Absolutely! Obviously, God knew I could do better as well and placed my girl Samantha as my instructor.

Most of you parents have experienced the "welcome home, I love you wag", especially when your kids were toddlers. You come home, the kid spots you and comes running to you as fast as they can to jump in your arms. You pick them up, swing them around and instantly get caught up in the moment. Yep, you are experiencing the "welcome home, I love you wag".

As dating couples, during the "romance" stage there may be some sightings or experiences of the “welcome home, I love you wag”. So many times, as a relationship grows, we get comfortable. We “expect” the partner to automatically feel the “wag” without the “welcome home, I love your energy and excitement. Why is that ok? We all deserve to feel loved and appreciated.

So here comes another miracle of Samantha. As a child with delays, her milestones happened and continue to happen when she is good and ready. In fact, they happen exactly at the time I need them. Interesting huh?

Think back for a moment in your life. How many times did we want to grow up and get the benefits that an older sibling or friend was getting, like driving a car or getting to go out with friends? How many times did we just want to be done with school and living the adult life with “freedom”? So many times, we are in a “hurry” to get to the next step in life before we are ready. We forget we need the training and maturity to be able to drive and hang out with friends responsibly. We do not realize we need the education to get a good paying job to have the freedom of living like an adult and paying bills for electric, water and food. All things happen for a reason, right?

Over the years. Sam's therapies typically consisted of an adult playing with her like a child. They would always use toys and games to motivate her to move, speak or do an activity of daily living like feed herself. Sometimes the therapists would ask her sister Haley, to join in. However, most of the time Sam was playing with an adult. So naturally you would think, like most children, she would learn to like the toys the therapists used to play with her and want them. Instead, Sam desired the adult play. You see it was not the toy or game that they played with that motivated Sam, it was the therapist, the adult, or her sister. It was the interaction and connection with the people_that motivated her.

When Sam was in music therapy, her therapist, would set Sam up on one side of the room, while she played and sang at the piano. Sam was around 4-5 years old and still not walking independently, but a crawling beast. Sam would be on her knees or bottom listening. The music therapist would be at the piano playing and singing an upbeat hello song. It went something like this “hell-lo Sam, hell-lo Sam, hell-lo Sam hello hello hello”. “Sam won't you play with me, play with me, play with me? Sam won't you play with me, bump da bump bump hello!” Sam would just smile and sometimes bounce to the beat. The therapist would look back at Sam watching her while still playing. Sam would, begin to force her body to get closer to the therapist's voice. She would scoot, wiggle, side crawl, etc. Sam would want so hard to follow the songs instructions and play however her body would fail her at times. Even facing those difficulties, her desire and determination was always there.

Many times, over the years I would experience the joy in Sam's eyes as "people" would come over to visit her or we would visit people. She lights up with the soul happy smile. She will just stare at them with pure love and excitement, just like the welcome home dog does. Her smile is so pure and full of gratitude and appreciation. It is like her core inner being is being filled up.

When people ask for gift ideas for her, I always say "people" or "time". Sam would prefer hanging out with family or friends over any material gift or toy. She gets so filled up from people.

She will often, daily, ask me “Debi, who's coming to see me today?”. Yea she calls me Debi. I pick my battles and that was never one of them, forcing her to call me Mom. She hears everyone else call me Debi so that is what she calls me. She is excellent at repeating what she hears. The good and the ugly.

Sam has this thing she does with me, that completely gives me the “welcome home, I love you wag”. She likes to ask me often, “Debi who's here right now?” We will list out all the family or friends’ names that are there at that moment. Sometimes, or most of the time her autism causes her to ask the same question repeatedly. As I am writing this, I am getting a revelation as to why she might ask so many times. Trust me, it can be asked like up to 100 times plus some. “Debi who's here right now?”

I am sure all of you who are autism parents can relate to the echolalia. What is echolalia? It is defined as the unsolicited and meaningless repetition (echoing) of another person's vocalizations, or speech. Sam repeats herself as well as others. However, I disagree with the "meaningless" part of the definition. I believe it is her way of expressing herself. We all learn to talk to ourselves silently and rationally to be patient and wait. Sam on the other hand, talks out loud and expresses whatever is being said in her mind.

She repeatedly asks "Debi who's here right now" until she gets the answer from me, she's looking for and then the "welcome home, I love you wag" begins. When she hears me answer "it's just me and you Sam". She stops in her tracks, takes a huge inward breathe of excitement and asks back with a huge smile. "Debi, it's just me and you right now?". I reply with “yep it's just me and you Sam”. She comes over to me, squares me up with her hands on my shoulders. She looks me straight in the eyes and says with all the soul love she has, “Debi, I just love when it's me and you don't you?” Then pulls me in with the best head tuck tight shoulder hug ever. I stop and allow these moments every time and always will. Just like you do when you stop and let the welcome home dog pour that love and happy on you.

No matter what kind of day I had, no matter how much stress is filling my mind, no matter how late I am at getting somewhere, when that happens, I get grounded in Sami love. Sami love is the purest form of innocent, forgiving, forever supportive and dependable love. Sami love anchors my core being to stop, allow and love. Let me say that again. Sami love anchors my core being to stop, allow and love.

How can a child with so many delays and underdeveloped brain function be able to get to my core being and heal me everywhere I hurt with a simple "I just love when it's me and you Debi"? She makes me feel special. She makes me feel important. She makes me feel like I matter. She makes me feel loved.

We all need and deserve to this feel way. Is it possible, we are presented with opportunities through our day to experience these kinds of feelings? Maybe it is through your child or pet? Maybe it is through a coworker of friend? Maybe it is your partner? Maybe it is nature? Maybe we need to be more open to where we are throughout the day and who around us can bless us or we can bless?

When Sam has visitors, she tends to locate the person whose energy is attracting her and saying to her spirit they need love. You will see Sam follow that person around. She will sit as close as possible to the person, almost in their lap. She will stare and smile at them as they talk with a look of Sami love and admiration.

Now think about that for a moment, what admiration that is. When I think of the word admiration, I think of mental and emotional experiences that lead to feeling admiration toward someone. How can Sam, without those experiences, have admiration for people like she does? I believe it is one of her many miracles she was born with.

It sure feels uplifting to have someone purely interested in you. Interested in you for who you are and not for what you can do for them. It is like she can see inside souls the love level and picks the low leveled people to shower love on that day.

So many times, I hear people say, that people will forget what you say, people will forget what you do, but people will never forget how you made them feel. What if we really paid attention to making people "feel" the love? I believe our world would have so much more happiness. Don't you?

The sunshine from Sam is to give each other, on a regular basis, "the welcome home, I love you wag". By taking the time to stop, slow down and feel the energy love levels around us, we will know who needs some love. Then all we must do is say yes and just do it. Shower others with love before our minds talk us out of it. It is a totally free gesture. A simple smile, hello, how are you and really listen to how they are. You see my friend, in the end, love is what it is all about.

Chapter Eight

It is Okay.

It is a busy morning; the time just keeps ticking and anxiety is building to beat the late demon. Rushing through the house to get lunches packed, breakfast prepared, and bags packed etc.

The sense of urgency to not be late is in the room yes. Does Samantha feel that urgency? If she does, it must make her slow down. Maybe your children do the same thing? The sense of urgency causes weights in their feet and a double up on the questions.

As I am packing her lunch, she is asking “who's coming today Debi”? Before I can answer that question, she is asking another question. “Who's taking me to the van Debi”? As I continue to concentrate on the tasks at hand, like we multi-tasking moms tend to do on a regular basis. Where we start one thing, stop, start another thing, stop, go back to the first thing, you feel me? As I continue to multitask, Samantha begins repeating the questions. “Who's coming today Debi”? “Who's taking me to the van Debi”? A whole 2 seconds go by, the repeat button is stuck, and Samantha increases her volume in asking the questions again. “Who's coming today Debi?” “Who's taking me to the van Debi”? Now even though she is repeating questions and has elevated her tone a bit she seriously just wants answers. So, I answer her quickly as I am still rushing around. “Sam, Haley is taking you to the van and Rachel is coming today”. Her face shows a sign of relief as she goes back to eating.

So now we move over to putting our socks and shoes on. She sits on the bottom step that goes upstairs. She begins to attempt to put her socks on while talking to herself. She's saying "we got to hurry, we don't want to miss the van, do we? No. We got to hurry."

Yes, she is repeating me. Isn't that what our children do? Repeat us. As I am still rushing around, I stop and walk over to her. I look at her feet to see the progress she has made with the socks. She has one sock inside out but, on her foot, and the other sock is in her hand and she is trying to pick the strings off it. She begins to tell me "Debi, these strings are bugging me". Not only do the strings "bug her" but she takes full authority in making sure any "string" or "tag" is pulled off. That is right pulled off! No matter what the item is, a tag or lingering string, it is means for disposal is Samantha's mind. Only problem is, she has yet, to learn how to use scissors. No worries though, she is strong enough to rip them off. Yes, I said rip. So, you can just imagine how many holes we have in shirts, on towels, blankets, and socks. So Of course, in my hustle and bustle I grab the sock, turn it right side in and put it on her foot. I correct the other sock as well. As I grab her shoes to put them on her, she asks "who's coming today Debi"? I reply, "Sam you know who's coming today, we just went over it". She said again "I'm sorry who's coming today Debi"? Bless her heart she really cannot recall. I reply, "Rachel is coming today". Samantha smiles big and says, "thank you Debi, I love Rachel, thank you".

So, I go back to my tasks at hand, grab her lunch and I come back to the stairs where she has taken her shoes off. I say "Samantha what are you doing? We do not want to be late, do we? Why did you take your shoes off?" She looks up at me with her big brown innocent eyes and says, "Debi there's something in my shoe". Now we are still not ready, and the van should be here any minute. I am beginning to feel anxious. I quickly take her shoe off and sure enough there is a sock tucked inside the tip of the shoe. Typically, when Samantha takes her shoes and socks off, she shoves the socks inside her shoes. I sometimes forget to check inside the shoe for those socks before I put her shoes on her. I start apologizing, "Samantha I'm so sorry I left the sock in your shoe". Sam looks up at me again and with a sincere smile says, "it's okay Debi, it's okay."

That is a type of moment that stops me in my tracks. I feel a peace come about me as this child who is delayed mentally has just given me instant forgiveness. She has not only forgiven me, but she also poured it on with love. "It's okay Debi." She stands up, squares my shoulders with her hands, and pulls me for the best hug ever as she repeats, "Debi, it's okay, Debi".

There I was all full of anxiety, rushing around as my heart rate increased, I could imagine my blood pressure elevated as well. I was caught up in the tasks and getting them done in time. I am certain the energy in the room was filling with anxiety as I put a sense of urgency out there. At the same time, Samantha was around that energy and it did not cause her to move any faster. What is interesting to me, is that her delays do not allow her to get caught up in worry, fret, doubt etc. Isn't it beautiful that she was and is able to be used to help us calm down? Our children, the ones we are supposed to teach, somehow teach us. If we are willing to be open to the teaching and allow it.

I know I am guilty way too often of causing the energy in the room to fill with my anxiety, with my fear or with my doubt. That energy may interfere with those in the room. I am certain some feel it and begin to look for what is stirring up emotion in the room. Others may never notice it and pay no attention to it. When I begin to feel the room energy turn negative, I start to search for the cause of it. Why? Because I feel uneasy. I feel distracted, I guess. Once I see the cause, I analyze the situation to determine if action needs taken.

I'm talking about a situation such as being in a room with coworkers. All the coworkers are working at their desks, in their own world trying to complete the tasks at hand. Suddenly, there is a power outage flicker. The lights flicker on and off several times. The computers begin to flash. Several beeping alarms begin to go off. Everyone stands up looks around and begins to see and investigate the situation. Many have their opinions. Several are frustrated about the work that did not get saved before the outage. Others are worrying about how to complete tasks to meet deadlines. Worry, doubt, fear, anxiety begin to fill the room. It gets so thick you feel like you could slice it.

What do we do? Sometimes the action is to escape the situation, so those negative emotions do not latch onto us. Sometimes escaping physically is not an option. Such as with Sam. She could not escape the anxiety and strife I was causing with the hurry attitude. So, what did she do? Without even consciously knowing, she kept calm and continued to get clarity to help herself feel at peace. Then when I realized what I had done and apologized, she quickly hugged my guilt away. She poured on the love.

How many times are we in a situation where we have caused pain to someone from our action? Maybe we are upset inside about a complication we encountered. Suddenly, a child, spouse or co-worker comes into our space with all this happy energy and attempts to chat with us and share some fun or smiles. We are annoyed because they interrupted our thoughts, and we are preoccupied. So, we are short, uninviting and may even lash out with some harsh words. Ever been then? I know have done just that several times in my life. I have learned to start identifying it not only because of Sam but because of Haley as well.

Many times, I would pick Haley up from school with all the weight of the workday burdens on my mind. She would get in the car, happy to be out of school, ready to start sharing her day and asking for things from me. At that moment, I would lash out with a mean, harsh, response loaded with tons of negative energy. Haley used to just soak up that energy, keep it inside and start blaming herself. Which we all know leads to mental strongholds and destruction. Thankfully, Haley learned how to identify these situations more quickly as she got older. To which I am incredibly grateful because she taught me as well.

I can remember the day I had the revelation of this type of forgiveness. I had picked her up from school again with tons of workday stress on my mind. As I lashed out with a harsh, mean response on this day, Haley put her hands into a "T" shape and said, "mom I call timeout". I was stopped instantly in my tracks, just like the morning with Sam and the socks. I said, "excuse me, timeout for what?" She said, "I call timeout because you are obviously upset about something and taking it out on me, so let's start over. What is bothering you mom, why are you so uptight?" I felt my heart drop to my toes as a large lump swelled up in my throat and I fought back tears. She was right. I was upset about something else and taking it out on her. She would quickly jump right in to getting me to vent my situation and feelings while putting her exciting day and all the good news aside. How did she learn to do that? How did she learn to be so in tune with others energy and feelings while at the same time put her wants and needs aside as she quickly offered a listening ear? She will tell you she learned how to forgive quickly from living with Sam. So many times, Sam would destroy her things, maybe there was a string or tag on it and the “rip” led to destruction. Maybe it was the time Sam threw her sippy cup out of the car window. Who knows when it happens? One thing is for sure, Haley learned it from Sam, and both taught it to me. They taught me how to forgive quickly and allow love to heal.

Some of the pains we have go very deeply and plant a seed of destroying emotions in our soul. These are emotions such as guilt, anger, doubt, distrust, hate, etc. Those seeds will grow and flourish into lifelong strongholds on us if we do not allow quick forgiveness. It is like a weed that grows inside of us. That weed grows into some stinking thinking that brews a crockpot of negativity the longer it is in us.

The sunshine from Sam is to forgive, forget and love quickly so the weed is destroyed, and the light can come in. You see, it is with the light, that beautiful things flourish and grow. What has happened that causes the stress and anxiety is exactly what is supposed to be happening to teach us and allow growth.

Chapter Nine

Hugs

It is early in the morning around 5:30 am. The sun is just starting to peak. I open the door to Samantha's room and the bells that hang on the doorknob jingle, as she begins to wake and stretch. Am I the only parent that still sees the baby in their grown children? Every time she does that morning stretch, I can see the little toddler in her and I just want to pick her up and squeeze her.

Samantha's door has bells hanging on the knob. The bells look like a string of bells from Santa Claus's sleigh. It was Mamaw Dots idea to put these jingle bells on her door. The purpose was so that if Samantha woke up in the middle of the night, the bells would wake me so I could get to her before she walks near any steps. Her visual impairment prevents her from seeing centrally and disrupts her depth perception. So, stairs have always been a huge safety concern.

In addition to the bells, I have a baby video monitor even though she is in her twenties. The bells are an added sense of security. We all know that us mothers and most women strive to feel "safe" right?

You see, Samantha has a history of sleep walking. That is right, sleep walking. Around the age of 12 years old is when I first noticed it. Now remember she had only learned to walk without a walker around the age of 11. Imagine your newly walking toddler, but in a teenage size body, walking in their sleep near stairs. It was like I was watching a very unsteady tight rope act about to go bad.

Our blended family started learning new rules and routine in our home. One of them was to make your bed every day. Sam learned to do this as well. In fact, Sam is probably the child that follows the rules and cleans up after herself the best. I must give that credit to my husband. He is particularly good at keeping a house clean and making it a daily routine, so it is never a huge chore. Sam tends to learn best by example because she is more of a visual learner. I love to hear her say "show me Debi".

When Sam would sleepwalk, she would get up, make her bed, and walk to the door. As she opened it, the bells would slam against the door causing a jingle. That jingle would be heard on the video monitor and cause me to almost jump out of my skin ready to put a fire out. You know the type of wake up where you are asking yourself, wait where am I? What is today? What is happening? I would see on the monitor she was up and at the door. I would typically sprint to her door but sometimes It would just be a fast walk. The goal was to get to her before she got to the stairs. You may be wondering why I did not have a gate at the top of the stairs to prevent her from being harmed from them? I did for a while, as did most of you probably too, right? Never did I imagine I would need a gate for a lifetime though. The years of the gate rubbing on the wall would break it down and cause damage to the wall. So, we decided the gate was going to go and we would use the video monitor and bells to help instead.

As I made my way to her, I could see that her eyes were closed as she was walking toward the bathroom. She was not even trying to feel for the banister or the wall. Remember, she is a new walker who has the steadiness of a tightrope walker about to go bad. I would grab her hand and direct her to the bathroom. She would use the bathroom while her eyes were still closed and not answer any of my questions. There was silence, just silence. I could not get her to wake up most of the time until we were back at her bed. I would try to get her back in bed to go to sleep. Typically, these events happened way before time to get up. On average, the time was around 1am – 3am. You feel me, right? It is at that moment that I would start counting the hours for hope that maybe I could still get a couple hours of sleep in before the alarm would go off. No such luck for me. As I would attempt to raise her leg to get back into bed, she would wake up and become like a stiff board preventing me from bending her knee. I knew right then, my day was going to start and getting any more sleep was off the list. Goodbye to the hope of more sleep. My alarm has officially gone off already.

On these mornings I had two choices, get angry over something I could not control or get a head start on the day and make it great day. It did not take me long to become a morning person and choose to get a head start on the day. To get the disappointment out of my soul and anger out of my mind, I had to get one of Sam's cleansing hugs.

When Sam hugs you, she does more than just politely hugs you. She squares you up, gives you a sweet smile, pulls you in while she tucks her head on your shoulder. Then she holds on for some time. She may even rub her hand on your back or pat it. If you are sad and crying, she will say "it's okay".

Samantha will now stay in bed until someone comes in to get her up. That has been a training in process for over 20 years. She rarely sleepwalks any longer.

However, if she is out of her routine in anyway or there is a full moon her nights will get challenging. She will wake up early in the night ready to start the day. Lucky for me I am well trained for these moments and ready for my hug.

There are still moments I get close to that edge though and try to get her to go back to sleep. I go into her room ask her if she needs anything. She looks up at me with those big brown eyes and says "no". I ask, "do you need to go to the bathroom?" She responds, "no". I ask, "why are you pounding on your headboard?" She replies, "I'm sorry Debi". I explain it is the middle of the night. It is way too early to get up. I turn off the light, go back to my room and get all tucked in. At that moment as my eyes close, I hear the video monitor. Sam is talking to herself saying "it is way too early. It is not time to get up" It is as if she is coaching herself.

I instruct Sam every night that when she is ready to get up, all she must do is say "mommy come get me" and I will hear her on the video. I have been instructing this for like

5 years, however she chooses to hit the headboard instead or the wall. Then will remind herself, once she is up, that she needs to say, “mommy come get me”. She will repeat it over and over and even ask me, “is this what I say Debi?” and I instruct again, “yes.” However, we have not hit that milestone yet.

On a morning when she has slept well, I am fortunate to get one of Sam’s morning hugs and smiles. It is like the one I described earlier, the cleansing hug, however, it usually is followed by a double or triple squeeze of excitement to start her day. It is always followed with statements of starting her daily routine. She starts talking to herself. “I need to get dress and make my bed. I need to eat breakfast and pack my lunch”. Thanks to the autism characteristic of repetition, she will repeat this over and over until the tasks are completed. It is entertaining most days and needed as a reminder for me to stay within our time frames.

How good of a day would we all have if were to start each day with a cleansing hug and a decision to make it a great day?

Hugs are so simple, yet for some, extremely uncomfortable. The feeling of someone coming into their personal space like that is overwhelming and can even feel violating.

The sunshine from Sam is that hugging can be therapeutic and heal us in areas we never knew existed. Hugs can be cleansing and lift your spirits at the same time. Try it and feel the peace. Start with a child's hug.

Chapter Ten

Thankful

There are days I still mourn the loss of things I thought Samantha would experience. Such as, seeing her in a beautiful gown to go to a school dance. Seeing her have friendships where they do fun things together and have sleep overs. Seeing her drive her own car and earn her own money. I often wonder what extracurricular activity she would had enjoyed. With her love of music, I would think she would have been in the band or done something with music. I am certain she would have been in the "boy crazy" club. She is one big flirt and loves to find a "cutie pie" in every group she is in. As I watch many of my friends become empty nesters, I know I may not experience that either. Samantha is unable to be left alone and has not learned to care for herself yet. She always needs someone with her for safety reasons, like a toddler. For the rest of her life, she will need a caregiver. When these thoughts start to pop up, I can feel a flood about to happen. A roaring, powerful, strong flood of negativity and depression. Even right now, writing this section and seeing it on paper hurts. If I do not find a quick way to turn my frown upside down and find the good, I will spiral into a dark place. This is when I repeat in my spirit over and over, "all things work together for the good." In a matter of seconds, I can feel the peace take over with the fact that being Samantha's caregiver is an honor. I remind myself of all I was forced to learn from her and how thankful I am for those lessons. I start to uncover rocks and find the golden nuggets I get from being her "Debi". I switch my mind from expectations to appreciation. When I change the thought of "She will never…" to "I get to …", it is like the flood headed my way quickly detours. For example, "I get to" cuddle my baby forever. "I get to" have a spiritual being in my presence that grounds me. "I get to" hug her and fill up on her smile every day. I could go on and on of all the "I gets". Once I do this, it reminds me that she is exactly who she was designed to be and so am I.

I also watch Haley, mourn the loss of not having a typical sibling bond like I have with my sister. Haley has watched her triplet cousins and stepbrother & sister have those sibling connections. Even though she yearns for that type of relationship, she is unable to have that typical bond.

What sibling connection am I referring to? It is the built-in friend and sometimes best friend you have in your sibling. They experience the parental discipline with you, the family trips, and memories. They play with you, hang out with you, and help you when you are hurting physically, emotionally, or mentally. I cannot remember how many times my sister was there for me. A listening ear when I was frustrated, a hand to hold when I was afraid and an amazing protector when anyone tried to hurt me. My sister is always just a phone call away. It is an overwhelming feeling of comfort, knowing your sibling has your back forever.

When Haley was in high school and not old enough to drive yet, she would be fascinated when older siblings would drive and pick up the younger sibling. In her mind that was so cool, and it always caught her attention when it was happening. She knew in her heart, Sam would never show up in her own car to pick her up from school due to her disabilities.

My niece, Cortney, use to be Sam's aide. She would care for her when I was at work. One day, I was late to pick up Haley and called Cortney to see if she could pick her up. There Haley sat in the front of the school building expecting me to show up in my mom car. Wow was she blown away when her cousin showed up in one of the coolest cars ever. The music was jamming as Haley ran to the car full of excitement. She opened the door to see Sam in the back seat. Sure enough, it WAS happening. Her older sister, with the help of her cousin, was picking her up. Haley expected nothing and to this day loves to share this story with appreciation.

Haley has missed and continues to mourn the loss of that type of sibling connection. However, she does get a sibling connection like no other with Sam. She still gets all the same things, just in a Sam kind of way. She gets the emotional and mental support. She gets to hang out with her and play with her. She gets an amazing listener in Sam as well.

When Haley needs some “bonding”, she will get in Sam’s world by cuddling with her or playing with her. Even though these are more toddler type games and activities, they still provide special sister bonding time. Haley will also take her out as if she were a teenage friend to visit people, do some shopping or just hang out. Taking Sam out is not an easy task either. Imagine all the things needed to be done to take a toddler out, except the toddler is in an adult body. Planning must first be done. How long will the outing take? What meals/snacks will be needed while they are out? Sam is on a soft diet to prevent seizures. Crunchy foods can trigger seizures, so packing food is easier and safer. Plus, her meds she takes for seizures might need to be packed as well if they will be due while they are out. Then there is the putting on of her shoes, coat or jacket and packing the backpack/diaper bag. Sam is not in diapers however she may get her clothes wet or have an occasional accident in her pants, hence the reason we need a backpack. If her clothes get wet from maybe a dribble of water, the shirt will need to be changed promptly before Sam decides to take it off. She has accomplished the skill of taking her shirt off. Sometimes she gets it wrapped around her neck, but she certainly gets it off without any embarrassment of being "nakey" as she says. I promise you that if the backpack is not taken, an accident almost always happens. I am certain you parents can relate to that.

I just adore the way Haley sees Sam though. I am so proud of the way she takes responsibility for her protection and wellbeing. She does not see Sam's limits. Haley looks for and sees potential in her sister.

One day, when Sam was around 7 or 8 years old, while we were in the backyard playing, Haley decided Sam needed to try the trampoline. "Trampoline?!?" I yelled as a question. She wanted her to get on the trampoline that did not have a barrier around it. All I could see was an accident waiting to happen. I could feel my heart race as Haley got on the trampoline and started jumping and flipping. The thought of Sam getting on the trampoline too totally had the overprotective momma bear coming out. Haley kept trying to convince me to let her try it. I kept saying no, as the anxiety was elevating to an all-time high. I now know this type of reaction, to an anticipated harmful event, is caused from catastrophic fear. What is catastrophic fear you may be wondering? It is ruminating about irrational, worst-case outcomes.

Without hesitation, Haley said, "mom Sam will love it and she deserves to bounce too".

My heart felt like a double-edged sword just went right through it. I knew she was right, and I had to overcome this fear and allow Sam to experience and grow. So thankful Haley was persistent. Why? Because Sam got on that trampoline and started bouncing on her knees and never fell off. I can still hear the belly laughing coming from them in my mind. We would then make "bouncing" on the trampoline a daily reward. Little did I know, that bouncing was building her stomach muscles that would prepare her to eventually get out of the wheelchair and walk on her own. See, everything happens for reason if we just allow it.

Sam is nothing but honest. I mean she does not even know how to be untruthful. She only knows truth. An unconditional love beyond measure. An instant rise in happy hormones with a hug or a simple I love you. No matter what day it is or how Sam feels, if someone wants to cuddle Sam is all in. I often think if we could all just be like Sam life would be more pleasant.

We all know people will disappoint and life will bring storms and pain. There is no way around this so learning to allow it and overcome the emotional pain will always bring the sunshine. But how do we do that? More importantly, how do we do it quickly, so we do not spiral to a dark place? We do it by being thankful through the disappointment.

What is disappointment? Disappointment can describe anything that crushes your hopes, ruins your day, or otherwise lets you down.

So many times, I watch disappointment happen to Samantha. Yet, she never allows it to attach to her. Samantha absolutely loves people. She often says, "people make me happy". The way she says "happy" will always put a smile on your face. She raises her voice in a cute, sweet, high tone with a big smile and says “happy” with all her soul.

Often on the weekends or holidays when her day program is closed, she will ask me “Debi who’s coming today?” When I tell her the name of the person or persons that are coming, you better believe it, she will ask all day until the time arrives. She says, “who’s coming today Debi?” When I tell her, she replies with “what time are they coming Debi?” Now what is ironic about that, is Sam cannot read a clock or tell time however she will always ask “what time are they coming Debi?” She then grabs her notebook of paper and scribbles a note, that only she can understand, about the people coming and the time they are coming. Samantha has not met the milestone of reading or writing, yet. She may never read and write the way most of us do. However, she still scribbles and understands what she has wrote. When I ask her what it says, she is always able to tell me. After about 10-15 minutes she has already forgotten the answer and what she scribbled and will ask again. “Who is coming today Debi?” Once I remind her of who is coming, she will say “oh yea that is right, I am so excited.” She will smile big, shrug & shimmy her shoulders while she hugs herself. “Thank you, Debi.”

This back-and-forth questioning literally goes on every 10-15 minutes until the person arrives. There are times when the plans change. Just like in most of our lives, right? Plans change and we must shift. Well, when I tell Samantha that the person is not coming you can see the disappointment on her face, and she will say “that makes me sad.” She will ask if we can call them. If that is not possible or they do not answer she will say “I just love them so much Debi." She uses love to cover the disappointment.

How many times in our lives have we been disappointed and carried around the sadness for hours, days and even years? Some of our disappointments are deeply rooted in us and the pain is unmeasurable. It is unfortunate that whatever happened to cause that pain has happened for sure. One thing is for certain though, it has happened, it caused the pain and there is nothing that can be done now. Nothing. We cannot erase history although some of us are hurt so bad we purposely forget it. We tuck it way down in our souls and carry it with us, sometimes for life. All that carrying will eventually get heavy and weigh us down into a deep dark place. Then the hurt from the pain, deep within us, causes us to hurt others. So why are we carrying the past pains? What if we let the sunshine in and released the past?

The sunshine from Sam is to love and be thankful. We all know that hurting people hurt people. We also know people will disappoint. Expectations lead to frustration; however, appreciation and love can heal us everywhere we hurt. So, expect nothing and appreciate everything.

Author Bio

Debi Fideli-Robinson is the founder of 5 Pillars of Health & Wellness, where personalized health & wellness plans are designed using DNA. In addition, they also provide health advocacy & wellness accountability.

She is a health & wellness nurse with over 20 years of nursing experience. That experience has been in intensive care, emergency, maternity, geriatrics, home care and advocacy. She has been caring and advocating for her adult daughter, with special needs, for over 20 years. Through those years she educated herself on whatever was necessary to provide the best quality of life for her child.

She is quick to lend a hand and currently volunteers on two boards; a senior care community and a nonprofit foundation that raises money for scholarships & school programs. She also helps a local organization that feeds the homeless.

Debi currently lives in Ohio with her husband and daughter, Samantha. She also has a younger daughter, Haley who is a cosmetologist with an entrepreneurial drive.

Debi enjoys spending time with friends and family and hearing life's stories while celebrating and experiencing the little things. She always has a smile on her face and finds the glass half full of sunshine in any life storm.

https://debi-rn.com/

Special Thank You

As I began allowing the story of Sam & I to fill these pages, I knew proofreading and correcting grammar was going to be needed. I began asking around to see if anyone could recommend someone that might be interested in that task. I came up empty until one day, as I was working out with a dear friend on a health & wellness journey, it came up in my spirit to ask her. I kept getting this nudge in my gut to ask her if she would be open to reviewing my book. I mean she has been a teacher at Milford Schools for years and well respected in her professional career. I would always be drawn into her stories of excitement about her students and what she got to do that day. For those that know me, they will tell you I am not shy. I quickly wanted to get that gut wrenching feeling to ask her, to go away, so I blurted it out. “Would you be open to proofreading my book for errors?” She replied without hesitation, “I would be honored”. I was so excited! The proofing began and I would send her each chapter as I completed it.

I would like to give a special thank you to Kristi Jones, who volunteered her time and mind to review this book as I was preparing each chapter. As she would send back her corrections, she would always add words of encouragement. Her heart is a pure one and it is an honor to be her friend. Thank you so much Kristi!

Together We Can Make A Change

Samantha deferred her diploma when it was time to graduate at the age of 18. Luckily, we lived in a state that allowed this. Deferring a diploma means the student is choosing to stay in school beyond the typical senior year to obtain more educational development. Samantha was on an IEP and had not reached developmental milestones. This qualified her to defer her diploma until the age of 22. An IEP is an individualized education plan for students with disabilities to grow and learn based on their abilities. What a blessing this was for Samantha to attend the deferral program at her school. She was on a roll with the development of her activities of daily living and transitioning would only cause regression at the age of 18.

During her 4 years of extended education in the deferral program, Sam continued to learn skills to live outside of high school. When she finally hit the age 22, we had to transition. She was unable to do a job or go to college as she still always needed one on one care. We began searching for day programs. The choices were limited as there were not many adult day programs that accepted adults with developmental disabilities. Samantha was blessed to be on a state waiver that would pay for her to attend day programs. All we had to do was find the one that accepted her waiver and fit her goals for development. We were extremely fortunate to find a program that fit.

It was then I realized how unfortunate it was for those students that did not have the waiver nor the ability to do a job yet. Where would they go for continued development? Who would have to pay for that service? For

12 years these students attend a state public school and receive regulated yet individualized education with the mission of "no kid left behind". Well until the age of 22, then, sadly, they get "left behind." As most parents of a 22-year-old plan for a college graduation, these parents are planning for daily care of their adult child. It breaks my heart. Why isn't there a scholarship or post high school program for these children? There should be for sure. There are so many scholarships available and most of them are related to academics, athletics, minorities etc. However, there are none that I could find related to helping an adult with disabilities attend day programs.

I began to think of ways to change this. I decided to write this book about all the ways I personally learned from my disabled child. As I wrote the book, I realized my lessons from Samantha could help others as well. Then I had a dream stir up in my spirit. What if we could raise money to give scholarships to graduates from the deferral program to attend a day program? What if they could go on to learn, grow & develop just like Sam and other typical college or trade school students do? It is my strongest wish to see Sam present a scholarship such as this.

Will you help us? Do you want to be a part of making a change in this world? All the proceeds from this book will go to benefit the nonprofit organization that will be distributing these scholarships. In addition, you can donate to the Milford Schools Foundation for the Samantha Sunshine Scholarship. Sam and I are also available to share this story with groups to encourage them to live their best lives through the sunshine. Does your place of employment, athletic team, or small group need some sunshine? We would love to bring it.

To Donate:

Go to this link.

https://www.milfordschoolsfoundation.org/donate

To purchase Samism Inspiration Cards (The sunshine from Sam is) or Shirts.

go to this link.

https://debi-rn.com/